Radical Acts

Unconventional Wisdom for Shaking Things Up

Written by Lee Ryan and Viv McWaters

Illustrations by Steve Chapman | @stevexoh

Book design and hand lettering
by Mary Campbell | marycampbelldesign.com

COpyriGHt

This book includes stories of real people and real situations that we
have experienced, as a part of our work and our own professional
development, in a variety of industries around the world.

Published Independently by Beyond the Edge
ISBN 9798861025980

CONTENTS

INTRODUCTION

"I BELIEVE that THE MOST IMPORTANT single Thing. Beyond Discipline and creativity, is DARING to DARE."

- Maya Angelou

There are so many calls for change. From grassroots activists to civic leaders, a resounding chorus demands inclusivity, sustainability, and justice. Meanwhile in the business world we are supposed to be more agile, more resilient, and show more empathy, as well as align with organisational goals, and, almost inevitably, find ways to "do more with less". Change fatigue lies below the surface. People are exhausted, their vision narrowed. They are trying to survive.

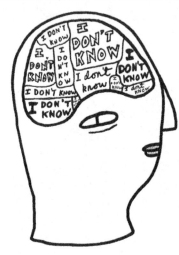

Under this stress, we try to think our way to solutions. Leaders are hunkering down and tightening their grip on strategy. We're in cognitive overload, with more PowerPoints to read and project plans to write than we seem to have time for. Instructional manuals are becoming increasingly literal.

But what if understanding the problem prevents us from discovering new ways forward?

Creativity and practicing art provide solace, lightening the world a little. People can see more, make connections and create some aliveness, for themselves and others. We propose radical acts that shake things up as a way forward.

And what if the most radical acts are deceptively small and intimate? More about motivating and paying real attention in a time-starved world. What might this look like? How might we begin to experiment?

We continue to learn from the indigenous people who live on the lands we now walk on. I was introduced to wayfinding leadership, says Lee, through a local university, and have returned over the years to a beautiful article by Chellie Spiller, *Calling the Island to You*[1]. She tells a story about Professor Charles Royal of the University of Auckland, whose field was indigenous development. He mesmerised guests with a story about Pasifika navigators. For the purposes of navigation, Professor Royal explained,

"... the wayfinder would conceive of the waka as stationary, whilst the world slid past, much as a train passenger looking through a carriage window sees the world moving.

By staying 'still', wayfinders align to the star path at night, and adjust to the ocean swell by day. Steering is done through sensation as well as sight. They gain important information from observing

the tell-tale cloud formations that develop over high islands and over coral atolls and note their colour – islands with heavy vegetation produce a dark tinge and those with white sand give a brighter sheen. They also observe the frequencies of ocean swells that can help identify land as far as 90 kilometres away, and the flight paths of homing birds that return to land at night. Such navigation is not just about the stars, sun, clouds, swells, or the wind – it is based on a deep understanding of the relationships between them.

As the world continues to move past, the waka's destination island eventually appears on the horizon. The wayfinder continues to adjust to signs, possibly even changing direction in a dogleg fashion. The task of the wayfinder is to stay in communion with the unfolding processes of the surrounding world and by moving from stillness, bringing the island to them through "be-coming". Conversely the task of the Western navigator typically involves taking the most direct route possible, relying heavily on maps, sextant and compass to make landfall."

At the heart of this is a deeply relational understanding.

This book captures some of the wayfinding that works for us.
We share what has become a way of working: setting a creative
direction, making over 'aboutism',
and loosening people's brilliance.
We have been influenced by
indigenous knowledge; the arts
in general, particularly theatre,
poetry, comics, street art and
writing; our backgrounds and
experiences; the people and
organisations we have worked
with; by games and play; and by
nature and the environment. It is
a deeply relational understanding,
and we pay homage to those Pasifika wayfinders.

For us, Lee and Viv and Steve, this book is something we can do
together to bring into existence
what was not there before. It
is an antidote to boredom and
despondency. It is a way to gather
disparate thoughts and ideas, to
grapple with them, to consider
them, and see the world differently.

Do you remember the monkey
bars at your local playground? Kids still love them and that power
you feel from moving through the air, grabbing one bar in front
of you, letting go of the one behind and grabbing the next, legs
dangling, momentum sending you forward.

They are the perfect metaphor for this book and for radical acts.
You need that momentum. You need to let go before you can grab
what's ahead. You need to keep going. If you hesitate, you might
fall or just hang there with your arms getting increasingly tired.

It's a RADICAL ACT to let GO of one thing before TAKING HOLD of something new. LET'S EXPLORE that together.

How to use This Book

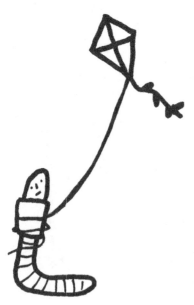

Using a radical act to shake things up is like flying a kite. You can find yourself struggling to keep the kite in the air, or unable to control it when the wind whisks it this way and that. Or it may be lying at your feet, earthbound because of a windless day. It might rip apart, or it might soar and delight.

When we talk about radical acts, we mean those things we can do to shake things up in a kindly, fun-loving way. We want to re-awaken our senses, explore a different take, and be inspired by the absurd.

We think these ideas might apply to you as an individual, and certainly to groups and teams, inside and outside of organisations. We have learnt this stuff by turning up to work with people and trying new things. Trying what we think might work, giving it a go, and modifying it on the fly as new information becomes available

We've divided the book into four parts.
Set a creative direction
Choose making over aboutism
Loosen people's brilliance
In the final section, we hand over to the creatures that co-inhabit this book. They tell us their favourite bits of wisdom.

You can start at the beginning, as most of us prefer. We've written it to read from the beginning to the end, not how a novel is written. But it flows in that direction.

OR YOU CAN DIVE
into a part That
attracts you.
That will work too.

SET a CREATIVE DIRECTION

" Creative people are curious, flexible _and_ independent with a TREMENDOUS SPIRIT _and_ LOVE of PLAY. "
-Henri Matisse

In our work we provide the gameplay, the rules and boundaries so that people can explore ideas and be creative within their field of expertise, to loosen their own brilliance.

We take risks to do new stuff, to break with convention, and not to be bound by unspoken covenants, because we know from our own experiences that we can wake up the brain by changing how things are done.

Lee came across Susan Newhouse who was leading extraordinary innovation workshops. She had just finished a piece of work on finding innovative ideas from everyday people in financial planning. I noticed she approached her design differently from other teams. She didn't immediately start populating a spreadsheet. She got the background material, sat in a chair, and thought about it. She would identify the essence of what people needed to do and turn that into a creative title, which I remember as "Walking on Thin Ice." She selected activities based on the focus and what she needed to accomplish.

This differed from others who talked about creativity and innovation but were wedded to a process. They would jump to what icebreaker they could use without thinking about what they were warming people up to do. We both worked for an organisation where people often asked for a handbook. I realised that Susan treated each workshop as a creative act. I look back at that time now and wonder if what would have worked is a creative apprenticeship of the type I found in writing programs that built creative confidence and skills.

• • • • • • •

If you want to set a creative direction for others, you will need to slay some of your demons first.

I grew up as a 'goody two shoes', says Viv, following rules and instructions, not wanting to cause any trouble or stress. I melted into the background, stayed out of trouble, and just got on with stuff. It was easier that way. Then I decided I wanted to do something unconventional for the times: "No thank you, nursing and teaching are not for me. I'd rather be a journalist, specifically, an agricultural journalist. And to do that I want to go to an agricultural college. I must continue with maths and science, not move to arts subjects."

The teacher I spoke to probably raised her eyebrows and tried to talk me into arts because I was okay with those subjects and barely managed with maths, physics and chemistry. And like a sheep being hoisted onto the boards for shearing, I did the only thing I could: I dug my heels in.

That's when I learnt about unspoken rules.
Girls don't become agricultural journalists. Yeah, right.

• • • • • • •

Our friend Izzy Gesell, an American humourist, speaker and improviser, taught us an important lesson about games. We were playing a game called Slap, Clap, Snap. We stood in a circle and our task was to create a rhythm using hands and thighs. Two slaps on the front of our thighs, two claps, then two snaps. It was easy to create a rhythm. Then it got complicated. Izzy would point to one person who had to say a word on the second snap of the fingers: slap-slap, clap-clap, snap-cat. Then the person on the left has until the second snap to come up with a new word that begins with the last letter of

the previous player's word. Player 2 might say tomato. And so it would continue. Slap-slap, clap-clap, snap-onion. Slap-slap, clap-clap, snap-net. Slap-slap, clap-clap, snap-tiger.

I loved that game, says Viv. Still do. I'm not naturally rhythmic so I had to concentrate on the physical part while paying attention to what people were saying. And I loved the different ways people played the game – some just dived in and had fun, others agonised over the word they would say, sometimes someone would freeze, sometimes the whole game would fall apart, and some wanted to restart, others to do something else.

We talked about how the game revealed how our choices affect at least one other person. Did we choose an easy word for the next player, or try to trick them? Over a drink in the bar later, Izzy talked about how you play the game is how you are in life.

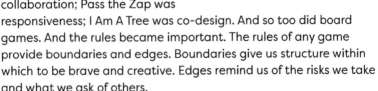

This was such a revelation, and like many revelations, it is obvious once you know.

Games became part of our repertoire. Physical games made the abstract more concrete: Group Juggling was collaboration; Pass the Zap was responsiveness; I Am A Tree was co-design. And so too did board games. And the rules became important. The rules of any game provide boundaries and edges. Boundaries give us structure within which to be brave and creative. Edges remind us of the risks we take and what we ask of others.

Boundaries and edges shape a creative direction. It can be small, like a game, or the shape of a week-long retreat.

Another revelation. Rob Daviau and Matt Leacock brought out Pandemic Legacy on the back of the popular cooperative game Pandemic. Cooperative games were a bit edgy; most people thought board games were competitive, and most were. Pandemic Legacy is also cooperative and, as described by Matt Leacock, breaks a whole bunch of board game covenants – unspoken rules about how board games are 'supposed' to be. Playing cards are torn apart and discarded, the board becomes covered with stickers, roles disappear, and the game can only be played once.

This time, it became clear to us that there were many unspoken rules – covenants - and not just about girls becoming agricultural journalists, but about workshops and meetings too. Rules that no-one questions. Like having an agenda, doing a round of introductions, sitting at tables, and having an expert talk with a (bad) PowerPoint. These all became acceptable, because

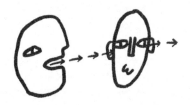

at some level, we understood that that's how things are done. But what if they're not? What if we remove the tables, find other ways to discover who is in the room, and let people talk about what they know?

What if we put ourselves in the shoes of the participants? We all know what that is like because we are participants at some time or another. What if we notice the things that don't work and think of other ways to do that? That is part of setting a creative direction.

• • • • • • •

I met Pablo Saurez at an improv conference in Amsterdam, says
Viv. He sat with me at lunch after more than one person had
said we should talk. Apart from improv, our paths merged with
our work with humanitarians.

Little did I know how much
Pablo would become an
influence on me and my
work. Pablo is an example
to all of us of the power of
experimenting and learning
alongside the groups he
supports. He noticed that the
conventional approach of
telling people about the risks
of climate change did not
impact their actions enough.

Pablo wanted to break some
conventions and covenants.
He designed a game where
people had to choose whether to pay for climate data. The
game had no climate data, just resources represented by beans.
Decisions to be made are represented by dice throwing and
assessing the odds, commitment is represented by standing
up or staying seated, and consequences of our decisions are
represented by payments of more beans depending on the
outcome. The game reveals a lot about how willing you are to
take risks.

HOW YOU PLAY THE GAME IS THE WAY YOU ARE IN LIFE.

There's that voice, saying, "But it's just a game, it's not real life. I think I would act differently in real life."

Would you?

"But it won't work with my team, in my organisation, with the Board, or with scientists, social workers and the local arts cooperative," says just about everyone.

Pablo likes to share the story about using a frisbee in the United States Congress to highlight the random and devastating impacts of climate change on communities worldwide. He is as much at home using these approaches in the corridors of power as in the villages in developing countries. It's a testament to taking a radically different approach to a conventional problem.

• • • • • •

I couldn't work out what was happening, says Viv. I was running the final day of a three-day workshop with about 30 scientists. The first two days were conventional sciency-type things: presentations, posters, Q and A, people sitting at round tables scrolling through their phones and aliveness appearing during the breaks and at the end of the day in the bar.

There was a couch and a large potted indoor plant. It was very green - the plant, not the couch. I was hunkered down behind the couch. Hiding. My pulse was racing. I could barely breathe. My brain had stopped working, the amygdala taking over and proposing that the only option was to hide, which is what I was doing. When my heart rate steadied, my breathing relaxed, and my amygdala released control of my brain, I stood up to see the consequences.

No one had noticed I was missing. No one saw my panic attack. They were too busy having animated conversations and writing up ideas. Someone walked past me and said, "This is great. Don't know why we didn't do it for the whole three days."

I'd broken with convention. I'd woken up people's brains by changing how things were done. It was not without its risks. I had no idea what would happen after two conventional previous days. Hence, my panic attack was caused by making conclusions based on observation alone. I introduced a day of Open Space by removing the tables and having the scientists sit in a circle. The agenda for the day was blank. I walked around the circle explaining the Open Space process. I invited the scientists to propose any relevant topic, step into the circle, grab paper, write down their ideas, announce them aloud, and post them on the agenda wall. After the first person went through this process, a deluge of other ideas and offers quickly followed. I said, "It's all up to you now, see you at 3pm," and walked out of the room. That's when the panic set in. As I walked out, people were still sitting, watching me, waiting for me to do something else. I knew that Open Space was self-organising: it always worked and was the best fit for this group. What I saw, though, was blank faces and accusatory stares. My brain jumped from observation to conclusion and panicked.

That's an extreme example. I don't usually suffer panic attacks, but it was a reminder that taking risks is not without risks. It was also a reminder to stay curious, to recognise how easy it is to see something and then jump to a conclusion. The missing parts are analysing and interpreting, which often need questions asked and answers heard.

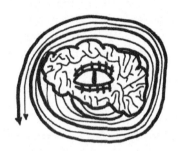

On the other side of curiosity is a hunch. Here, we risk contradicting ourselves but hang in there. Being curious and trusting your hunches go hand in hand.

Stories are an integral part of Playback Theatre, a form of improvised theatre that relies on audience stories. As novice performers, says Viv, we were listening to the teller's story, and before we played it back to the teller and the audience, our instructor told us to 'trust your hunch'.

This is shorthand for 'trust your hunch about what's not said' - a particular listening skill akin to curiosity.

We edit ourselves. We leave stuff out, because we think it's uninteresting, irrelevant, or too personal. This is why we love the colour/advance activity. When someone is telling a story, a listener can give one of two instructions: to 'colour' a part of the story, add more detail, or to 'advance', move the story forward. It's such fabulous, real-time feedback.

We get it. Taking risks to do new stuff can be a big ask. It's easy to stick with convention. But as a leader we set a creative direction by how we set up, show up, and get people up and moving. It's what we need more of to break through those unspoken rules, the covenants, that keep us stuck.

What does this look like practically? When designing we begin with constraints: How many people? How long? Where? What do they want to do? We ask many questions and listen for the shift from what people think they want to when they start talking about what's really going on. Remember trusting your hunch? We do that. We try to figure out what people are not saying.

Then we start shaping (refining comes later) remembering that boundaries or shapes give us the structure to be brave and creative, and edges remind us of the risks we take and what we ask of others.

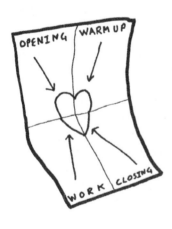

We fold paper, or play with stickies, we let our ideas roam about until they settle. Like Susan Newhouse, we sit in a chair and think about the workshop. This helps us avoid the traffic lights trap.

The traffic lights trap, where lights switch on and off due to automated timing and not because of whatever mess is piling up, can happen for anyone caught up in abstract ideas and content. You can spot it when icebreakers are used without knowing how they might, or might not, be warming people up to do whatever it is they need.

We avoid putting together a set of activities in a green-light-red-light sequence by grounding ourselves in the design, using folded paper, stickies, drawings, and jottings. We try to reduce  everyone's noise, fostering air, light, and space. Discovering what's at the heart of a workshop helps us connect with the creative direction.

• • • • • • •

Setting a creative direction is many things. It's seeing the need for a shift. It's being willing to try something different and sometimes to be the first to do so. It's about shaking loose ideas and sensing what might work. It's about visualising the experience others will have. There's no formula. There's no timeframe. Creativity doesn't show up on demand.

It's a radical act because we sometimes don't know where we will end up, and do it anyway.

CHOOSE
making over
ABOUTISM

"Go and make INTERESTING mistakes,
make AMAZING mistakes make, Glorious
and Fantastic mistakes. BREAK RULES.
Leave the world more interesting
for your Being Here."

Neil Gaiman

When doing some post-graduate studies, says Viv, I enrolled in a subject called Ways of Knowing. I was intrigued. I'd grown up in an era where knowledge was power, information was king, and all you needed to do was accumulate enough. The idea that there were different ways of knowing meant I wanted to know more. Meta, eh? How do Arctic Terns know how to navigate from one end of the planet to the other? How do indigenous peoples know where to find water?

We are overwhelmed with information.

There's an epidemic of aboutism, the tendency to tell, to talk about doing something rather than doing it. We're all guilty. The trick is to catch ourselves. There are times when aboutism is okay too. If I'm telling you about my latest holiday, you are probably happy to just listen to me talk about it rather than recreate the experience in interpretive dance.

There's an expectation that knowing about something will make it useful, or relevant, or usable. It will change our minds, what we do, how we vote, and where we spend our money. Yet we know that there are other ways of knowing. Our gut, bodies, and feelings might give us different information. We might expect one thing, and hope for another.

Aboutism lets us off the hook. While talking about something, we are avoiding *doing* something. An example is asking questions about an activity. We introduce a group activity, usually with just enough information to get people started, and someone wants to ask a question. We avoid questions because we know that, while well-intentioned, the question is just a way of mitigating risk, avoiding doing something they have not done before. If we skip questions and let people start they usually figure it out. That's what we mean when we say choose making over aboutism.

We're fans of popcorn Power Point as a way of avoiding aboutism. It's an idea we got from our improvisation friends where we make a deck of, say, 50 image-rich slides. We ask the audience to choose five of them randomly. We'll go to those slides and say whatever comes to mind, usually a story. The other 45 slides remain a mystery, maybe piquing their  curiosity to find out more. Instead of using a pre-prepared script to talk about our topic, we are challenged to improvise and tell stories.

I was recently involved with designing and facilitating a citizen assembly on the future of water for a city in New Zealand, says Lee. There was complicated information provided by experts and some options to choose from. We needed to get people inside the options. We designed activities where we asked people to put any two options together and see the benefits and drawbacks, not to find the perfect combination but to try out a combination and see what they learned from it. Then, we asked them to try a different combination and notice what they learned. It's easy to get stuck into listening to experts talk about solutions or wanting to find the perfect answer. Sometimes, we need activities that bridge the challenge and potential solutions so people can be a bit more experimental and thoughtful.

Musicians don't start by sitting around exchanging information. They begin by playing. They discover stuff about themselves and each other through play. Band members can do solo work. They can team up with others inside and outside the band. We've often considered bands a good model for working together and collaborating. We should all be more like bands.

Artists are good at avoiding aboutism. Rather than talk about their art, they make art. They keep making art until something happens. Painters paint, illustrators draw, musicians play, writers write.

There's a show on British television that illustrates this. It's called *Portrait Artist of the Year*. Different artists, amateur and professional, are invited to paint a portrait of a well-known person in four hours. It is filmed live. The artists get on with painting, bringing their own approach and style. Some start with painting straight onto a canvas. Others take photos. Others do an

outline in pencil. And the judges provide commentary about what's happening. While the artists are making, the judges are engaged in aboutism. While talking about the art is their job, it's a good reminder of the difference.

"But I'm not an artist!" Which is a good time to point out the difference between artists and being creative. Artists choose to be an artist as their profession, whereas anyone can be creative.

Being creative is a radical act when it's outside the realm of artists. Being creative and making art is a way of avoiding aboutism.

• • • • • • •

When we work alongside people who don't consider themselves artists we use activities to encourage their innate creativity to emerge. Storytelling, for example. When we work with indigenous groups, we see the power and the potential for all people to be storytellers and to connect to their own stories of tūpuna or ancestors. This storytelling might be accompanied by dance, or drawing, or simply walking.

Everyone can tell their own story, make their own map and for others to hear and see what that map means. It's the telling of stories and making maps that connect us. Art becomes a touchstone.

When people grapple with a task or a problem, it is not devoid of talk. People connect better when they are doing a shared activity. And the activity doesn't even need to be

relevant. Doing something with our hands - kneading bread, making a model, painting - keeps one part of our brain busy while another part can talk and make connections.

Have you ever been in that situation where you are struggling with a problem, turning it over in your head, trying to figure out a next step, or simply to understand what's happening? And then you call someone and start talking about it. Your brain races ahead, and you can see clearly what needs to happen next. The difference is you have spoken out loud rather than silently toss ideas about. We call this playtesting, an idea from game design, and incorporate it into our work. When you have an idea, it usually makes perfect sense until you try and explain it or do it. This is playtesting – taking an idea and trying it out.

WA WA HA MY HEAD HAS FALLEN OFF

We were standing in a circle, eager to start playing the next game, a new one that none of us had played before. It sounded fun, but the more it was described, the less fun it became. There were lots of instructions about what to do when and if a particular thing happened. At one point, somebody said, "Can we just play it instead of talking about it?" That's playtesting.

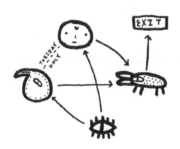

There's a simple group activity that reveals the importance of playtesting. You ask small groups to come up with a variation on the game Rock, Paper, Scissors. Some groups talk about how they might do a variation. Others play different variations. Those who play with their ideas instead of only imagining how they will play come up with better variations. This describes one of our favourite sayings by Richard Pascale[2], "It's easier to act your way into a new way of thinking, than to think your way into a new way of acting."

Whatever we are thinking makes perfect sense in our heads. Like those variations of Rock, Paper, Scissors, they rarely survive the journey from brain to action. Flaws in our thinking become immediately apparent when we playtest.

• • • • • •

Dance with the unknown, the unexpected, the strange, the creatively risky. Don't be lulled into the warm embrace of aboutism.

I realised this when I finally attended a writing workshop with Dark Angels, says Lee. It was an introductory day, and I managed to grab the last spot. I turned up at Strawberry Hill House, a curious architectural wonder, both Georgian and Gothic, nestled in a well-to-do London suburb. I came with, as asked, my favourite novel. I spent way too much time deciding which one book was my favourite.

That day, I discovered that with a few prompts, people could write paragraphs in the style of cherished novelists, in ways that were indistinguishable from the originals.

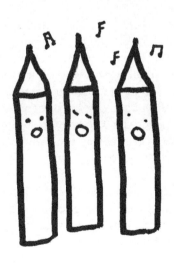

The lesson was as profound as it was simple: true art, which vibrates with life and speaks to our souls, lives in the act of creation itself, not in the discussion about what type of story it was.

And what truly stirs better writing into being? It's not the earnest lectures, not the ivory tower of theory. It's the act of creating - words on the page, recording the first few minutes of a podcast with music in the background, doodles on a napkin. I have attended many workshops and webinars, and bought books about storytelling. Still, nothing matched the activity in a room of writing for 10 minutes the opening paragraph of someone else's favourite novel. Making.

• • • • • • •

Sarah Ruhl[3] says, "Why are umbrellas so pleasing to watch on stage? The illusion of being outside and being under the eternal sky is created by a real object. A metaphor of limitlessness is created by the very limit of an actual umbrella indoors. Cosmology is brought low by the temporary shelter of the individual against water. The sight of an umbrella makes us want to feel both wet and dry: the presence of rain, and the dryness of shelter. The umbrella is real on stage, and the rain is a fiction."

We're curious about workshops and meetings and conferences and how so much of what is in the room is flat and two-dimensional. The post-it note, the flat surfaces of the white flipchart paper or whiteboard, and the projector screen. What happens when we bring out a set of Muji pens, drawing paper, art cards or hand-made wooden name badges? People notice the care.

When designing and delivering workshops, we pay attention to the materials - how they look, how they feel, and if they will work. We all appreciate beautiful materials, pens that sit nicely in your hand, colours that sing, and cards with that all-important feel. When we use popcorn PowerPoint we fill small individual cups with popcorn. Necessary? No. Appreciated? Yes. These gestures and objects send messages. They say you are worth working with.

Beautiful materials are worth the investment.

• • • • • •

The first pancake always goes in the bin.

This is one of those irrefutable and inexplicable facts of life. Anyone who has made pancakes knows that the first one is rubbish. We know we expect the first pancake to be rubbish, just like our ideas and art. Photographers take 100s, even 1000s, of photos to get just the one brilliant image. We continue to hope though that our first idea will be our best. Instead of talking about our one brilliant idea, be more like Steve, our illustrator who makes 100s of drawings for us to choose from.

Making and art are at the heart of being human, of being connected. Making and art are at the heart of avoiding aboutism. Of hope triumphing over expectation. And of different ways of knowing about ourselves and the world.

Loosen People's Brilliance

> Thus, the task is NOT so much to see WHAT NO ONE yet HAS seen, BUT TO THINK what nobody yet has THOUGHT about that which EVERYBODY sees."
>
> — ARTHUR SCHOPENHAUER

Imagine a conference in Singapore, in one of those big shiny hotels. The public spaces are all glass and chrome and neat as a pin. Stepping outside into the lush gardens you notice the heat and humidity. Inside it's so cool the locals walk around with shawls and jackets to keep warm.

I'd come to share what I had learned about using improvisation in workshops, says Viv. The organisers were uncertain why I wanted a large space with just a circle of chairs. No tables. No lectern. No presentation. In only 90 minutes with 50 or so people we played some games that brought to life the principles that underpin spontaneity, being able to respond to something unexpected, even unimaginable.

Towards the end of the session, I set the group a challenge. They were to use improv in small groups to come up with a theme, slogan and a jingle for next year's conference. They had exactly five minutes. They were initially sceptical that such a task could be done, but five minutes later, they were surprised and delighted by their own creativity and ideas. Loosening people's brilliance happens when we set a creative challenge and put people to work. And for us, being brave enough not to be sure about what might happen next.

• • • • • •

Viola Spolin had a gift for understanding how to lift performance from both individuals and teams. She liked to solve a problem with a problem. You can't always give people direct instructions to solve a problem, but you can give them a focus that will help solve a problem.

The idea of solving a problem with a problem has stayed with me as potentially useful for groups, says Lee. I was working with a team where trust had been savaged by a leadership team member who had behaved badly with staff and clients. The board and the employees were disconnected from each other and found it hard to get going even though that person had left the organisation. I ran a session where we made a representation of both the current organisation and the future using LEGO bricks. While people were busy focusing on making and telling their own stories of what had gone on inside the organisation, the shared talk time built back, piece by piece, trust and a shared perspective.

• • • • • •

Groups and teams, even families, get locked into patterns. Our job is to help them discover their brilliance.

A group of very smart people who are defensive, holding tightly to control of the 'pen' and resistant to other thoughts or perspectives become siloed. Trying to help by telling them lots of stuff is tempting. We have learned to flip the workshop so people experience a new way. A collaborative team makes more progress.

I was working with a policy team, says Lee, who had already finished their first phase of looking at data and interviewing people to understand their policy problem. In a series of four half-day workshops, we used creative techniques to look at the problem differently. They needed a whole system map, and I noticed their current map was already very complicated. I took a creative risk. In an empty room, I gave each person a piece of lovely blank art paper and asked them to choose a coloured pen. They had 10 minutes to individually draw how they saw the system, showing the main parts.

I noticed that people generally find it hard to pay attention to information. So, on a hunch, I asked them, as their colleagues talked in turn about their drawing of the system, to write what they loved most about what this picture showed about the system. We then had some different diagrams and what worked about each of these. In exploring what they learned from the activity, they distilled insights about the system and what they learned from each other.

As they reflected on their time together, they said that they felt 'looser', encouraging open-mindedness. They realised they generated more insights than working alone and went further and faster than when using conventional approaches. They worked in bite-sized chunks, which meant they got to deeper ideas. Shared thinking 'in the open' built on and revealed differing perspectives. They discovered as a group, they were brilliant, and they could work with their complementary working styles and strengths.

This is about groups working together. The process helps them creatively and lightly to make progress, to have their own insights and discoveries.

Our challenge is to come at this obliquely. Asking people directly to be brilliant hardly ever works. Gently nudging them to loosen and reveal their own brilliance nearly always works. In this we are inspired by poetry.

I first came across Emily Dickinson's poetry in my 20s, says Lee. It's bewitching. I wasn't always sure I grasped everything in her poems, but I was captivated by her writing. I have also noticed how her oblique and distinctive poetry continues to appeal to a wide range of people. It does not seem to date. It allows space for different generations to find meaning and beauty.

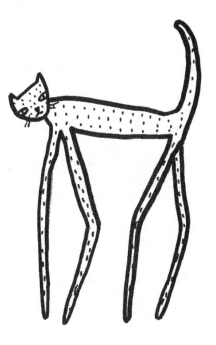

It was the second day of training a group of coaches who work with leadership teams. Instead of opening with a recap, I used Surrealist Q & A, which we learned from Doug Shaw, says Lee. The group was sitting in a circle of chairs. I handed them some blank cards and asked them to write a one-sentence question they were sitting with from the previous day that started with the word *why*. I then asked them on the back to write a one-sentence answer which started with the word *because* - however, the because answer should relate to an entirely different topic.

One person asked their question, and the next person read their answer. What we saw was that all the questions sat in the space without having to be directly answered. We didn't need to solve

or answer their question for them. This activity enables us to sit with the messy realities of where we are at with any topic. There were moments of laughter with answers that either made no sense or were just funny. Then there were the tiny insights where there is a collective indrawn breath when a question and an answer collide.

We can shake up conventional thinking and open new pathways for understanding. Oblique approaches can stimulate more in-depth conversations that help us puzzle through meaning by unpacking its layers to reach underlying truths.

When I think about Emily Dickinson's poem[4] and our work, "Tell the truth but tell it slant" captures our challenge to be bold. To inject a radical act and to sit with the mess rather than a tightly controlled, prepacked format that provides no oxygen or light for the conversations that need to happen.

"...but tell it slant" allows us to turn a problem sideways and give people a chance to find their way into the truth. Wayfinding. This means suspending the need to explain, to get people to do the work without signalling that it is being done. Telling it slant, lets people arrive at their own truths through a process of discovery.

The opposite of the 'tell it slant' approach is the deadening, zombie event. The hero doesn't notice the zombies and it turns out heroes can't outrun zombies. The relentless march of aboutism tramples everyone in its way. There is superhuman strength in these decaying bodies. This is the same with covenants. We follow these even when they don't result in what we need people to feel - more alive, more connected and more inspired by each other.

WISDOM OF
the Creatures

"You know," said Arthur, "It's
at times like this, when I'm
TRAPPED in a VOGON AIRLOCK with
a man from Betelgeuse, and
about to DIE of asphyxiation
in DEEP SPACE that I really
wish I'd listened to what my
mother told me when I was
young"

"WHY, what did she tell you?"

"I don't know. I didn't listen."

-Douglas Adams

Many lovely creatures have been along
for the journey. We asked them what they
would like to say in this final section.

Connection before content. Humans are beguiled by expertise. Don't just talk about the importance of connection and relationships, do it at the start of every event. If you find you are still talking at people 40 minutes into an event then you have fallen into the expertise trap.

Boundaries give us structure within which to be brave and creative. Edges remind us of the risks we take and what we ask of others.

Dollops of content are easier to
digest than great slabs.

Set a creative direction. Continue
to learn, experiment and take
small risks, improvise with people,
and stay alive to the possibilities
in the moment.

Just enough lines to get ideas flying...
Say what you need to say, then stop
without elaborating or explaining. Trust
that you have said enough.

Use WORDS that DANCE.

Charles Mingus says: "Making the simple complicated is commonplace; making the complicated simple, awesomely simple, that's creativity."

Plain words speak louder
than dense incomprehensible
language. See what I did there?

Dance with the unknown, the
unexpected, the strange, the creatively
risky. Don't be lulled into the warm
embrace of aboutism.

"The Truth must DAZZLE GRadually"

Often, it's more meaningful for people to gradually unearth the truth in their own time and in their own way. Avoid metaphorically battering people with truths you or others think they need to hear.

Wake up the brain by changing how things are done. Vary the type of thinking and responses. Avoid post-it thinking where all the thoughts are the length of a bullet point.

MAKE STUFF.

Find new and interesting ways
for groups to make connections.
Draw, dance, create stories and
maps, take photos - whatever art
stretches people.

DON'T Conflate POLITENESS with AGREEMENT.

Choose kindness over judgement.
Everyone has something going on
in their lives.

Let people struggle, but give
them time to grapple with ideas,
information and decisions.

Don't fall for the icebreaker trap. If it doesn't contribute to the heart of a workshop or event, choose something else.

People are energised when we move, as humans are meant to do. Even small movements energise us.

over to you.
your turn.

Radical Acts: Unconventional Wisdom for Shaking Things Up

To @stevexoh for saying yes to illustrating our book based on some vague thoughts.

To Johnnie Moore whose raised eyebrow or crinkled brow and razor-sharp insights had more influence on this book than he probably knows. And for some timely editing.

To Mary Campbell for her inspired design.

To our colleagues and friends who question, challenge, and generally support our projects, even the unfinished ones.

To all the people who have attended, and contributed to, our workshops and events, online and in-person.

To Mike and Pete. Just because.

iNSPIRatiON

1. Spiller, Chellie (2016) *Calling the Island to You: Becoming a Wayfinding Leader*, University of Auckland Business Review

2. Richard T. Pascale, Mark Millemann, and Linda Gioja, *"Changing the Way We Change,"* Harvard Business Review 75, no. 6 (1997): 126-139.

3. Ruhl, Sarah (2015) *100 Essays I Don't Have Time to Write: On Umbrellas and Sword Fights, Parades and Dogs, Fire Alarms, Children and Theatre*

4. *The Poems of Emily Dickinson: Reading Edition* (the Belknap Press of Harvard University Press, 1998) Tell all the truth but tell it slant - (1263)

Adams, Douglas (2002) *The Ultimate Hitchhiker's Guide to the Galaxy*, Random House, New York

Gaiman, Neil (2018) *Art Matters*, Headline Publishing Group, London

Gesell, Izzy (1997) *Playing Along: 37 Group Learning Activities Borrowed from Improvisational Theater*, Whole Person Associates, Duluth

Owen, Harrison (1992) *Open Space Technology*, Abbott Publishing, Potomac

Poynton, Robert (2022) *Do Improvise*, The Do Book Company

Spolin, Viola (1999) *Improvisation for the Theater* (Third Edition), Northwestern University Press, Evanston

Rob Daviau and Matt Leacock: Pandemic and Pandemic Legacy (board games)

The State of Legacy with Rob Daviau and Matt Leacock | Game Chat
https://www.youtube.com/watch?v=s0yIY5K2zS8

Pablo Saurez: Paying for Predictions interactive game
https://www.climatecentre.org/games/2501/paying-for-predictions/

Melbourne Playback Theatre Company
https://melbourneplayback.com.au

Portrait Artist of the Year (2013 - present) Storyvault Films
https://www.imdb.com/title/tt4445396/

Dark Angels: Creative Writing for Business
https://darkangelswriters.com/

Johnnie Moore (2023) *Unhurried: What's Possible Beyond Busyness?* https://www.unhurried.org/book

Steve Chapman @stevexoh (2023) *What the February?*
https://www.wtfeb.com

ABOUT US

Lee Ryan

Lee Ryan loves it when she can help people discover their own brilliance. She led the facilitation of Aotearoa's first citizen assembly, and codesigned events on the edges - Radical Acts, Policy by Design, Design for Social Innovation, and on topics as diverse as inclusion and diversity, policy development, and climate change.

Lee also has the world's best dog, Mac, who is still training her in the art of stick throwing.

Viv McWaters

Viv McWaters is a facilitator, trainer, and bird watcher based in Bells Beach, Australia. She mixes science, arts, and a dash of improvisation to transform mundane meetings into dynamic experiences.

Viv is at her most inspired when teetering on the edge of the unfamiliar, constantly discovering new ways to engage, connect, and surprise. Or when searching for street art.

Steve Chapman

Steve Chapman (aka @stevexoh) is an artist, writer and speaker based in London, UK. He makes distinctive black and white drawings, colourful paintings, street art and his weird conceptual art projects such as Sound of Silence - the world's first silent podcast featuring special guests.

His now legendary "(Not a) Lost Cat" poster has been spotted in 54 countries across every continent (including Antarctica).

Steve is at his best when he is not quite sure what he is doing.

Find out more about Radical Acts at RADACTS.SUBSTACK.COM

Printed in Great Britain
by Amazon

29642765R00036